Student Leadership 101:

101 Quick Tips So That You Can Lead So Others Will Happily Follow

For all up-and-coming student
leaders who want quick solutions
for helping a diverse team to be
who they are, at their best.

Crystal Jonas

ISBN: 9780976934462

LCCN: 2006901113

Text editing by Dan Sieck
Cover and text design by Janet Bergin, empoweryourawesomeness.com

The student on the book's cover is the author's son, Tyler Jonas Castro.
He got his hair cut not once, but twice for this picture!
Thanks, Puppy. Love, Mom

© Crystal Jonas

Crystal Jonas, M.A.
Author and Speaker

To Book Crystal for your next event, call 719.291.0366.
For a list of our most requested programs, please visit,
CollegeLifeSite.com Crystal will customize the program to
meet your needs and interests.

Also by Crystal Jonas:

"College Success Your Way: What Your Professors
Won't Tell You and Your Friends Don't Know"
– a book

"Student Success 101: 101 Helpful Tips So
That You Can Live a Rich and Happy Life"
- also a book

"Time Management 101: 101 Tested and True
Techniques to Take Charge of the Time of Your Life"
- another book

Dedication

This book is dedicated to Dan Sieck, an amazing man and a wonderful teacher.

Dan, through your work and your example you have made a powerful and positive difference in the lives of countless people.

The world is a better place because you are in it.

Crystal

Letter from the author

Dear Reader,

As a former Air Force officer, Assistant Professor and Academic Advisor at the US Air Force Academy, I appreciate and respect the value of student leaders in schools and in our society.

As a leader, you're in the position to touch the lives of many people and to help them to be who they are, at their best.

Yours is an important role and one few carry out well. I believe you have what it takes to be in the elite few.

The world is hungry for ethical, strong leadership. People need you to show the way. Read this book, and apply its guidance.

This book is part of my "Student 101 Series" and one of four I wrote just for you, the student who wants to achieve great results without having to spend your entire time in school figuring out how to do that.

Keep learning, because we leaders know that we are continually growing.

Now go make your difference in the world, and help those you lead make their difference too.

With warm regards,
Crystal Jonas
Manitou Springs, CO

Remember, Your Team is Watching You

When you're in charge, the whole group is noticing how you respond to situations, both good and bad.

Keep in mind that they are especially paying attention when the going gets tough. Leslie from the University of Florida had to remind herself of this when there was a project her group was working on and half the people weren't doing their share of the work. Nick from a university in Louisiana recalled this when his group thought they were going to get money to put on an event and it fell through at the last minute.

Look, all people can be at their best in good times. The test is how do you behave when the going gets tough?

When the going gets tough for your team, do you allow yourself to take part in any of the whining and hard feelings of the group? When you or a member of your team makes a mistake, do you vent? Or do you talk openly about lessons learned and move on?

This is tip alone is worth the price of this book. Remember that difficult times do not build character; they reveal it.

Your team looks to you for how to behave during difficult times. Stay calm when the going gets tough and they will come to respect you even more than they do now.

Be Clear About Your Team's Direction and Let Them in on It

Chris, a marketing major junior whom I met when I was on tour in California for my book "College Success Your Way," suggested that I include this point.

As the leader, you're responsible for letting your team know what the goals are. One of the biggest frustrations people have when they work in groups is that the leaders don't give clear guidance on what the target is.

Your team can't hit a bull's eye when they don't even know where the dartboard is.

State your goals clearly, and even consider posting them for all to see. People are very visual, and you can help them stay focused and motivated by having a clear picture of where they are now in reaching their goals, and how much further they have to go.

Lead by Example

Lisa, new to the Student Government Association at a Big Ten university wrote to me to say that from her first SGA meeting, she knew she was in a great organization.

"The president is always on time, on the point of the agenda, and respectful of every member of the SGA, even us freshmen!"

More than anything, how you act consistently will tell people the kind of person you are.

It so easy to talk about what should be done; it's quite another thing to actually do what should be done. People are noticing not what your words say, but what your actions say.

Lead by example and lead from the front.

What this means to you is consistently being on time to meetings (and by the way, end them on time, too), finish projects by the deadline, or before, and show respect to others.

Be Open to Off-the-Wall, Outside-the-Box Thinking and Ideas

Matthew, a sophomore at a small liberal arts college in the Midwest wrote me that whenever his Resident Life group gets together to solve problems, they start by playing creative games, like charades or categories. "It limbers up our brains," he wrote. "Then, we have a fun brainstorming session. We write out the question, like 'What's the best way to get more students involved in dorm activities?' and then we all toss out ideas. We get going really fast with all these off-the-wall answers. It's funny and fun. When we're done, we come back to all those ideas and start putting the best answers to work for us."

Who are we to squash brilliance that comes in unexpected forms? When you're brainstorming the best way to accomplish a goal or to solve a problem, keep it in the true spirit of a brainstorming session. Ideally, you'll have five to seven people, more is okay, if you must, but consider breaking the team into more than one group.

Put the question on the table. For example, you may want to ask, "What's the best way to raise money to hire a speaker for our group's next national conference?" Start the tape or digital recorder and let the ideas fly.

You'll come up with fun, crazy, brilliant ideas, and lots of them.

Focus on the Positive

Jennifer, a junior who will next year be the student in charge of Welcome Week for her college's incoming freshmen, said that the "positive factor" is the most important element that makes new students feel comfortable and happy they chose their school. "Every student on the Welcome Week committee was chosen for attitude first. It makes a huge difference in giving the new students a positive first impression of the school."

As you lead your team, keep your attitude upbeat whether it only meets for a few months a year, or for the better part of the entire year. Remember that these students are volunteers, and they have tons of responsibilities outside of this group.

Catch people in the act of being good, smart, funny, helpful, selfless, any value you'd like to reinforce. Praise them openly and be specific about what they did and how that helps to further the mission of the group.

When you are praising them, use their names, look them in the eye, and be sincere. It's amazing how you will find people going out of their way to do well when they know they are appreciated.

Frequent, prompt, and honest praise will go a long way in helping people stay on track when it seems that no one is noticing their contributions.

Stay focused on the all the great unique talents your people bring to the group and they will continue to live up to your high expectations.

Put Thanks in Writing

Simple courtesies help you make a positive, powerful impression in the workplace. This is a gracious action that will distinguish you with your peers and your supervisors, both with the teams you lead in school and in the future,

Not only can you praise people in public, you can send a thank you note as well. How rare it is to get a thank you note these days, especially those that come through snail mail. So few people take the time to send these. If you do, you will be admired and respected.

Again, say exactly what you're praising the person for and how it helps your team.

It's also a great idea to openly praise people in front of others. Again, always make sure your comments are sincere and focused on a specific action.

You know another really special thing to do? Send a thank you note to this person's parents. Your thoughtful actions will become legendary. So few people think enough to even say "thanks" anymore, much less to express their thanks in writing.

Share Compliments

A participant in one of my seminars that I give for college groups called "College to Career Jumpstart" told me he doesn't like to get compliments, and told his boss where he had a summer intern job not to bother because they aren't necessary.

Wrong attitude. Always graciously accept a compliment.

Especially troublesome in this particular example is that this man was part of a team of 12 people who accomplished the task he was being complimented for. So the compliment wasn't just for him, it was also for his team!

Allow people to say nice things about your work any time they want. Just make sure your share that compliment and say something like "Thank you! The team put a lot of thought into it. I will be sure to pass your comments on to them."

Not only is that the gracious thing to do, it's what a true leader would do.

This takes away nothing from you, by the way. The average person knows that it's because of your leadership that the team was able to reach such stellar results in the first place.

Focus on Solutions, Not Excuses

Be solution focused and you will be unique among your classmates and in the corporate world. Too few people think about how to solve a problem. They'd rather just sit around and complain about it. And I'll bet you know plenty of people who are really good at complaining, don't you?

True leaders are willing to do things others aren't.

One thing they're willing to do is to not sit around whining about what went wrong and whose fault it is. A key to leadership is to always give to the team credit for any great feat they accomplished, and also take the hit when something they do goes less than great. Your standing up and taking the blow will earn you many loyalty points.

Take responsibility for your leadership. Learn from the experience and move on.

Let others see and hear you staying solution focused.

Discuss the problem only long enough to define it so that you can move onward and upward.

Anyone moving forward will make mistakes. The key question is how quickly do you recover?

Delegate

If you're like most of the students who go to my college success programs, you are busy! You go to class, you do homework, you might be in study groups, you have your organizations and associations that you volunteer to serve on, and you probably have a job, too. That's a lot of responsibility!

Don't try to do all the work yourself.

There are three main reasons for this. First, you don't have the time to do everything yourself. Second, you are not, nor do you need to be, great at everything. That's what leadership is for. Find the best person who would be naturally perfect for the job and delegate the task to him or her. Third, when you delegate work to others, you show that you trust them to do well in that job.

Most people do not like to be micromanaged. You know what that's like. Your boss gives you something to do and then hovers over you, asking questions about how it's going every five minutes, giving you ideas on how best to do it.

So, once you do turn over the task to someone else, get out of the way and don't micromanage.

Your success rises and falls with your ability to lead people. As you follow this tip, make sure that you are choosing the right person for the job. Allow your people to play to their strengths and to take on duties where they will naturally shine.

They will appreciate the faith you place in them and the respect you show them by asking them to take part in the project.

Play to Team's Strengths

When you delegate make sure you're assigning tasks based on the strengths of your team.

Let's say you've got a task that involves interacting with the local radio stations. Not a good idea to ask your biggest introvert to take this on, when clearly this is a job for your gregarious extrovert. Save that wonderful and quiet worker for a behind the scenes role.

Make sure you listen, watch, and pay attention to not only what each team member enjoys doing, but also what she's actually good at.

Here are some questions to ask yourself when choosing the right person for the right job. Does the job require

Someone who works better with people or with paper?

An idea generator or a maintainer?

A short-term or a long-term commitment?

A creative thinker or a literal thinker?

A veteran or a newbie?

When you assign tasks to people, let them know that you thought of them for that job because you've seen how well they've done in similar responsibilities. Your belief in them will bolster their self-esteem and research has shown us that people tend to live up to our expectations of them.

Be Flexible in Your Approach

Have a clear-cut, well-defined goal, and make sure you are open and flexible in how you reach that goal.

If you have a "high-performance" team, then it's even more important that you get their input into how to achieve these goals.

High-performance teams are made up of people who know their jobs well, and have a clear idea of what's expected of them. They have a firm grasp about the task at hand, but are not necessarily the best students at school.

If you want your team to buy into your goals, then you'll want to get them to buy in early. Do this by asking their opinions on the best way to accomplish the goal.

Naturally, if you're asking their opinions, you're going to want to make sure that you are implementing their ideas as much as possible. This is where your flexibility comes in. You'll want to be open to adding your team's ideas to the mix, so you can't go into the project thinking that there's one way to do it and that's your way. You've got to be willing to trust that you're not the only one with great ideas on how to get things done.

Establish SMART Goals

Many schools request my goal-setting workshop for their students, so if your school would also like to do this, go to CrystalJonas.com/College_Programs. You'll find my contact information there. Please note that this program is available through special request only.

Let your team know your SMART goals. They can use this process for anything from a long-term goal of graduating with a certain GPA, to a short-term goal like the best way to make your groups' next fund-raiser a shining success.

Specific – Precisely describe the goal. Remember, they must know exactly where the target is in order to hit it.

Measurable – Quantify your goals. This inspires people to stay on track because they can readily see how far they've come, and how much further they have to go.

Attainable – Aim high, but not so high that the objective is unreachable. If you want to stretch your group, ask their opinion, and get their agreement. Do reserve the right for you as a team to revisit the goals and set new objectives as necessary.

Realistic – Has the objective been reached before? If not, you may want to take a second look.

Time limit – Have a date when your goals will be met. The old saying is that goals without a deadline are just dreams.

Expand Your Network

Use collaboration to your advantage. You aren't the only leader in your organization or association. Hook up with others and brainstorm "best practices" together.

Working together, you are much more powerful than any one of you would be individually.

Putting your heads together allows you to share common concerns and learn from the mistakes of others. Sure beats making all those mistakes yourself!

Also, you can run ideas by this group before presenting them to your own team. This will help you troubleshoot and iron out some problems before you reveal your ideas to the team.

You'll seem (and be) much smarter and well prepared when it's time to bring your ideas to your team if you've had a chance to run them by your network first.

Inspire Others to Motivate Themselves

Here's my philosophy of leadership. Leaders are stewards of talent. As such, their charge is to see the best in people and help them be who they are at their best.

There's a philosophy that suggests that we cannot motivate others; they can only motivate themselves.

What we can do, though, is to see the diamond in the rough and to hold up a mirror to people in our team, reflecting what's best in them.

Help others to be who they are at their best and they will amaze you with their ability to stay focused and consistently be at their personal best.

Show Confidence in Your Team

Let people know that you believe in their ability to bring their best to the table.

This means delegating as appropriate and getting out of their way while they do the work.

It also means that you ask their opinion and actually be willing to incorporate their ideas into your processes. Not many things make leaders lose credibility faster than asking for opinions they have no intention of using.

People who feel valued motivate themselves to be at their best. They need much less supervision from you.

Tell them "I believe in you." "You can do it." "You've done well before, and you will do well again this time." "Your best is good enough."

Show Excitement for and Commitment to Your Goals

Let your passion for your vision for the team come through. It's been said that enthusiasm is contagious and if you're genuinely excited about your team's goals, they will be much more likely to follow you.

Allow your actions to support the fact that you wholeheartedly stand behind the team's goals. This will be crucial when the going gets tough. And if your goals are at all challenging and exciting, it's not likely to be smooth sailing the whole way.

Your team needs to know that you are dedicated to seeing through the process of growing and achieving. Stay focused on the outcome and how to get there.

They will see this determination in you and will be influenced by it in a positive way.

Be Results Oriented

How many hours, days, even weeks have been lost for lack of a leader who will keep the team on track and concentrated on the outcome they do want and not the problems at hand?

Now, this is not to say that you ignore or refuse to discuss problems, just keep a handle on the course of discussion.

Let people know that there will be a time to discuss the problem so it can be clearly defined. Specifically, what would make a better outcome happen in the future? What could each person do to make sure that happens?

Problem solving should be no more than 10% discussing the problem; the other 90% should be spent planning the solution.

You may be pleasantly surprised at how quickly this skill can be modeled by your team. With you leading the way for how to respond to problems, they will quickly catch on that your team is results-, not problem-, focused.

Maintain Positive Expectations

Read all the self-help books and communication guides you like and you will find time and again the fact that we get what we expect, from ourselves and from others.

Maintain laser-guided focus on what you do want to happen. Make your spoken and nonverbal language clearly convey that you have absolute faith and conviction that the positive outcome you've discussed as a team will come to pass.

When you need to correct your course, remind yourself of the goal, adjust your approach, and set your sails once again for the shore, positive in your expectation that you will reach the point you desire.

Remember Others

Your team is probably overworked and certainly under-paid, right?

You will build trust and loyalty among your people if you remember them and get to know them as individuals and not just members of the SGA or the student newspaper.

When people do speak to you, you need to remember what they say, so you can build your relationship with them.

When you talk to people, listen carefully to what they say. People reveal more that you might imagine. They will open up and tell you exactly what's important to them.

All you need to do to cultivate relationships with them is to listen and remember what they've told you, and reference it in future conversations.

You'll be amazed at how flattered people are that you remember them and how much more loyal they will be to you.

Help Your Team Grow Personally

There's an old saying that "people don't care how much you know until they know how much you care."

The members of your team aren't just worker bees; they have full lives of their own. Most people want to be successful; they just have no idea how to do it.

You could be the person to take a personal interest in what's truly important to your team. Guide them and encourage them to aspire to be who they are at their best.

In balancing their lives with personal growth and professional development, not only are they happy and fulfilled, they will be even more inspired to help you fulfill your vision for the team.

Everyone wins.

Remember What's Important to Them

Funny how people think that others are so hard to figure out.

Most people will tell you precisely what you need to know to connect with them on a personal level. All you have to do is listen.

To be a really good listener, you pay attention not only to the words, but to the emotions behind the words. Ask then how they feel about what they're talking about. Are they happy, excited, concerned?

Notice that this tip starts with "remember" what's important to them. The operative word is remember.

Okay, so you listen well, and they open up to you. Can you remember it later so you can follow up with them on it? If your mind is sieve-like and you tend to immediately brain dump everything that's not mission essential, you need to look at small talk in a new light.

What you learn during small talk actually is mission essential. If you know you'll soon forget what you've just discussed, keep one of those little spiral notebooks so you can jot a note about the person you spoke with, when, and what you discussed.

Extra important is noting when you'd like to follow up with them on this matter. They will appreciate your interest.

Tell the Truth, Even When It's Bad News

When I taught English at the Air Force Academy, one of my favorite of Shakespeare's plays was "Henry V."

Henry is about to lead his troops into battle and many of them aren't going to make it. Rather than sugarcoat what they're up against, Henry brings them together and lays it on the line.

He lets them know many will fall, and others will sustain injuries.

A downer, you say?

No. What he did was to immediately reinforce the greater cause they were all going to war for. He rallied them by renewing their passion and commitment for the greater goal they all shared. He also let them know their sacrifice would forever be remembered and make a difference.

So, when all is not well, continue to tell the truth. Look your team members square in the eye and tell the truth. Remind them of the goal, and that their work is important and makes a difference.

Know the Main Reason People Are Difficult

Before you go and put a label on people that may stand in your way of effective communication, know this. The main reason you see people as difficult is that they have a different style of communication from you.

Which means they probably see you as difficult, too.

What can you do to work with all different kinds of people? In general, people are motivated by the need to be right, the need to get the job done right, the need to be admired, and the need to be included.

If these motivators aren't satisfied, you're likely to have a difficult conversation on your hands.

So, how are you expected to know what motivates people? You guessed it. Listen to them.

Within moments, you will know what drives people and you'll be in a better position to help them be at their best.

Most people never learn this, or learn it and don't have the patience to apply the principle. Another chance for you to move onward and upward.

Cultivate the Top 20%

You've heard the 80/20 rule. Twenty percent of your people do eighty percent of the work, and there are countless other examples.

The way you can put the 80/20 rule to work for you is to remember that all team members won't be shining stars, nor do they need to be. And as focused and ambitious as you may be yourself, not everyone has your drive.

You can be sure you're directing your time, effort, and energy in its best place if you make sure you identify the top 20% who have the talent, drive, and interest in taking on more challenges.

Once you find them, foster their talent and let them shine. They will knock your socks off with what they can do for your team.

This is leadership at its best!

Ask Yourself the Ultimate Energy-Management Question

I teach students how to manage their energy, time and effort better so they can get better results for their investment. You can be more productive if you just follow optimal times to put forth effort.

Your greatest resource isn't your time, but your energy.

Each day, you're faced with innumerable opportunities to solve other people's problems, obsess, procrastinate, and in general, goof off.

It's easy to do any of these. We know, because we've done them all. To make sure you stay on track and do what matters most in the course of a day, you need to do a couple of things.

First, know what you want to accomplish that day, and second ask yourself what I call "the ultimate question." Throughout the day, whenever the phone rings, ask yourself, "At this moment, was I involved in a high-yield activity?"

High-yield activities are only those that get you closer to your goals. Only you know the answer to this question. Be honest. Often at first, you will find the answer will be "No, that wasn't a high-yield activity." Not a problem, simply decide if you'd like to correct your course, and if you would, do so immediately.

Choose Your Battles

I've had countless students tell me that they quit organizations in their schools just because there was so much back-biting within the team and the leaders did nothing to face it head on and stop it.

Not everything that happens in your group will make you happy. Sometimes people won't get along, or a project will fall behind schedule, or money you're expecting for funding just doesn't come through.

Watch what you choose to fight for. Make sure you moderate your level of intensity no matter what the issue, because your team will notice if you stay in control or not.

Not every issue is worth your extended time and attention, anyway. The "Serenity Prayer" works well here. Ask for the serenity to accept the things you can't change, the courage to change the things you can, and the wisdom to know the difference.

William James, the father of modern psychology wrote that the art of being wise is "the art of knowing what to overlook."

Make Wise Decisions the Ben Franklin Way

Your entire life is ahead of you. How to know what decisions to say yes, no, and maybe to?

It's not always easy to make a decision when you really have no way of knowing how it will all turn out. Sometimes you just have to be willing to examine all the information you have and then move forward.

You may find yourself stuck at a crossroads, not choosing one way or another just because you can't see down either road. Keep this in mind "Go as far as you can, and from there, you can see farther."

You see, you simply need a method for choosing the best choice at the time, and once you embark on that journey, you will gather more and more information and you'll be able to adjust accordingly.

To make your initial decision, do what Ben Franklin would do. Get a piece of paper and write your question at the top, then draw a line down the center. At the top of the left column, write "Pros", at the top of the right, write "Cons." Weigh one side against the other.

It worked for Franklin, and it will work for you.

Let Your Actions Reflect Your Priorities

If you're like most people I encounter in my Success seminars across the country, you occasionally do what's easiest before you do what's really important. See the back of the book for more.

Okay, does it happen more than once in a while? Well, take heart. You aren't alone, and there is a fix to this.

It's just a matter of acquiring a new habit. You need to make the conscious choice around how you spend your time.

First, you need to know what matters most to you, what your goals are, and your plans to achieve those goals. Now, that was said in one sentence, but when it comes to planning your life, you do need to put some thought into it.

So let's say you know what you want and now, it's time to get busy. Each day, you need clear direction on what will get you one step closer to your goal. Only you can determine if your actions are what I call "high-yield activities."

Be Aware That Time is Your Currency

When I'm talking with participants in my time management seminars, I tell them "No amount of time is enough if you don't know how you're going to spend it."

I often hear from my clients how they just don't have enough time in the day. I'll ask, "to do what, exactly?" Often the answer is something of high value, such as "to spend more time with my friends" or "to sit back and just listen to music."

And yet, if they are pressed, they would admit that throughout the day they had spent time on trivial matters, such as obsessing over something that happened long ago, long after the moment is over and the lesson has been learned. Or they may allow others to waste their time and let it go on because they won't set boundaries for fear of "hurting their feelings."

More often than not, the time passes without conscious regard for how it's being spent. Time is your currency, be aware of how you're spending it.

If you don't elevate many of your actions to purposeful decisions, you're likely to be spending most of your day on someone else's agenda, or worse, no agenda at all.

So you see, more time won't help you get more done. You need to make conscious choices and to spend your hours based on what matters most to you.

Walk Your Talk

You've known people who will say one thing and do another. Sadly, people will act in ways that contradict their ideals more often than they'd care to admit.

Do you say that it's important for your team to get along with each other and then allow Person A to bad mouth Person B when Person B is gone?

Why should your team strive to get along with each other if you don't model the behavior you expect?

Steven Covey, author of "7 Habits of Highly Effective People" wrote that we need to be "loyal to those who are absent." It's especially important that you stand up for anyone who is not there to stand up for himself.

Always ask yourself if your actions reflect your philosophy. As the old saying goes "Talk is cheap." And as I always say "People aren't listening to what you say, they are watching what you do."

If you value integrity, you must take a stand and stop gossip the moment you hear it.

Socrates said, "The first key to greatness is to be in reality what we appear to be."

Help Others to be Who They Are, at Their Best

Ralph Waldo Emerson wrote, "Our chief want in life is somebody who shall make us what we can be."

Do you see the best in others and reflect that back to them? One of the most significant contributions you can make to your team is to do just that.

So many people could be so much more if only there were someone who saw something special in them and helped them to cultivate those unique talents.

Your team is likely made up of a wide variety of people, some will be great no matter what you do, some will want to slide by with minimum input (or less) no matter what you do. And then there are all of those in the middle who will give their best to the team if only you see what's best in them and let them know you believe in them and appreciate their contributions.

The key is to look past their weaknesses as you focus on what their strengths are. It may surprise you to know that research reflects time and time again that behavior that's rewarded gets repeated.

This means that when you see someone doing what they do especially well, you'll want to make sure that that's given maximum attention, and you'll find that in rewarding the positive behavior, that same behavior gets repeated.

Even Temper Saves the Day

Some of you reading this are, by nature, easy-going. It's probably hard to ruffle your feathers, and it takes global catastrophe for there to be the slightest blip on your blood pressure reading.

If this describes you, you may skip this tip. If you're more prone to display emotions, give yourself some tough love here and own up to it, and then read on.

One of the hallmarks of your credibility, and your ability to positively persuade others is your ability to handle challenges. Not only do you need to be able to quickly problem solve, which you can, and that's why you're the leader, you also must do it with outward calm.

Here's why. Your team is highly tuned in to any emotional upheaval you may experience. If you're upset, put out, madder than heck, frustrated, whatever you may choose to call it, and you openly display that, they will notice and respond accordingly.

Do what you must to stay outwardly calm in times of challenge. Your best bet is to take a few deep breaths.

When you're stressed, your breath becomes shallow. If you don't feed your brain the fuel it needs to function, it isn't going to think those brilliant thoughts that allow you to solve that challenge and get on with business.

Let the Buck Stop with You

President Truman had a sign on his desk that read, "The buck stops here."

It's tempting to pass on problems to someone else, and to refuse to take responsibility for something, especially when it's so easy to blame someone else.

Stand up to the situation and let your team hear and see you take responsibility for anything the team has done that didn't quite work. Let them hear you say, "We tried, it didn't work. Let's talk about lessons learned and move forward."

If you alone made a decision that didn't pan out, be open about it. Here's what you learned, let's move onward and upward.

People absolutely know when you've messed up. Don't think for a minute you can hide that fact. You would look silly and weak. Now, I'm not suggesting you talk yourself blue apologizing. Just be open about it, and quickly move on to what happens next.

Leaders who don't take responsibility for their actions lose respect from their team. When respect is gone, you might as well pack it up and go home, because you surely have lost your clout to lead others.

Take Well-Advised Risks

In order for your team to create results that are better than any team has done before, obviously, you're going to have to do something differently.

Be willing to research, ask trusted advisors, ask your team's input and to make a decision to try new approaches.

You've heard that saying "If you keep doing what you've always done, you'll keep getting what you always got."

To break your team out into new horizons of success, you must be willing to take calculated risks and do things differently.

There is a caveat with this. Don't go into a team and try to change everything at once. They will not appreciate this approach. Find out what's working and keep it just as it is. Find out what slight changes would make measurable and positive differences, and take on those next. These are your best bet for immediate "wins."

Once you've got a win or two under your belt, go for more involved changes to improve the team's systems and processes.

And, of course, you know, involve the team early and often, you've got a lot of talent all around you. Make the most of it. All great leaders do.

Be Flexible

When you want your team to know you respect them, you will want to include them in decision-making. This means you can present an idea and expect for them to buy into it wholesale.

If your team is a high-performance team, this tip is even more important. After all, they are good at what they do. They know what works and what doesn't. They likely have many of their own ideas about what would make your processes and systems better.

If you bring in your ideas and expect there to be immediate excitement and buy in, you're probably going to be disappointed.

Yes, you do need to provide a clear vision of the ultimate goal, however, you'll want their input into the best way to get there.

When presenting an idea, make your bottom line clear, and be open to their ideas on the way to make it happen that's best for all.

Involve People in Changes That Affect Them

I'm often asked when I teach college leadership groups "How to Inspire, Manage, and Lead Teams" what the best way is to get people to get on board with change.

People naturally resist change, because it's an open acknowledgement that some aspect of their involvement with the group will be different from now on. Funny thing is, change is happening all the time, it's just when it's talked about, people tend to resist the process.

If you want people to be with you when the change is complete, involve them right from the start. Get their input in the early stages and they will be much more open to accept the result. And you'll have other ideas on where the potential flaws are so you can fix them before they snowball into mistakes of epic proportions.

The key here, get their input early and often. Change will be much smoother.

Be Clear About Why Change is Necessary

Too many new leaders take on their duties, find fault with the status quo and immediately want to make sweeping changes.

This annoys team members to no end.

It's not so much the changes themselves, it's that there seems to be no clear reason for the changes to happen.

First, when you're new to leading a team, even if you've lead before, if it's a new team you're leading, wait before changing anything. Look, listen, and observe group dynamics. Understand who is listened to, they are the people you want to address first. They are sometimes called connectors because the team goes to them for information.

Take these connectors aside and tell them you're thinking about improving a process (or whatever) and ask what they think would make it work. Make it clear to them why the change is necessary and then sit back and listen.

From this, you'll have plenty of information to anticipate what the rest of the team will need from you when you tell them why the change needs to occur.

Be Willing to Grow

The more you learn, the better you'll get both in terms of personal growth and professional development.

Keep reading business books and glean as much as you can from these resources. Also, read the biographies of leaders you admire. If there is a leader you've heard about whose style you would like to model, see if she or he has written a book themselves.

You'll benefit greatly from going directly to the source for guidance.

By the way, it's a hallmark of successful people that they keep learning. They read, listen to audios, and watch videos on leadership and personal growth at every opportunity. Perhaps this is why they continue to rise to the top of any group. So, don't think the education is over when you graduate. Successful people keep learning, growing, and evolving. Either keep up and move ahead, or you will be left behind.

Max Dupree, author of Leadership is an Art wrote, "In the end, it is important to remember that we cannot become what we need to be by remaining who we are."

Reach, learn, grow. You'll keep getting better.

Be Clear About Your Expectations

Are you clear about what you expect from your team? If you consistently feel frustrated because you tell them time and again what to do and they just don't do it, you must look at how you're telling them what to do.

F.F. Fournies, author of Coaching for Improved Work Performance writes that the number one reason people don't perform the way they should is that they don't know what it is that they are supposed to do.

When you reach your level, it's easy to forget that you have a huge body of knowledge that other people don't have. Make sure you're making your points clear and not assuming they have all the information you do.

Act Quickly on Good Ideas

I write about how important it is to make connections with your teachers and their points of contact in the business world and to follow up on them quickly.

Too many students have let great contacts slide because they'll ask for the names of people to contact for informational interviews, then they will never call! That could have been the first step in launching their dream careers!

Don't over think your great ideas. Move forward on them. Learn quickly, then move on again.

How many really great ideas have you had only to get stuck in analysis paralysis, or to be overwhelmed by other stuff that is busy work but not necessarily productive work?

Good ideas usually have a pretty short shelf life.

Be sure that you act quickly to set in motion ideas that you know are sound. Sure, you won't be able to accomplish the bigger projects in a day, but you can set down a tentative plan and begin making progress immediately.

Great leaders are decisive, action-taking people.

Norman Bushnell, the founder of Atari, said, "Everyone who has ever taken a shower has an idea. It's the person who gets out of the shower, dries off, and does something about it who makes a difference."

Help Your Team Members Solve Their Own Problems

Are you a good problem solver? You probably are. It's easy for your team members, once they learn that you're good at this, to bring you their problems more and more frequently.

Avoid this trap. Sure, there are times when you need to have a bit of involvement, and occasionally, you may need to be right smack in the middle of helping your team member iron out an issue.

However, if you make them dependent on you, you are turning yourself into a micromanager, and your team will never reach its true potential. Neither will you.

You must teach your team the process you use to solve problems so that they have another tool in their tool belt.

Until you help them to be largely independent of you, you'll never create the kind of synergy needed for a team to truly perform at its best.

Encourage Independence

This begins with encouraging them to solve their own problems by teaching them the questions to ask and the processes you use to come up with the best answers.

You also encourage independence when you ask them the best way to get to the clear-cut goals you articulate.

By fostering their independent thought, you are creating an atmosphere where you have several or many people with a wide variety of ideas and levels of experience to come up with grand solutions and approaches to getting business done in the best possible way.

This also helps you stay away from "group think" when the entire team gets the "yes, that's right" and "me, too" attitude. This attitude is the kiss of death to creative thinking.

Influence the Attitude of Your Team

You can have a measurable impact on your team's attitude by modeling the one you'd like them to adopt.

More than anyone, you as the leader will have an influence on how other people think of an idea, treat each other, and perceive the value of their work.

This is especially true when the going gets tough. If you have less than great news, you need to honestly deal with it, and then give a clear direction on how the team will manage with this new turn of events. They will be looking to you for how to think of this news.

You will determine whether they see it as catastrophic, a bit bad, or actually an opportunity in disguise. Direct them how to be by behaving the way you wish them to behave.

Recognize That Success is a Process

I've helped many people new to their student leadership positions over the hump of appreciating that progress takes time.

It's tempting for those of you experienced in leadership to think that change can happen quickly.

Remind yourself that you're not operating independently, and so much rides on the team you're leading. Yes, they will take guidance from you, however they are still individuals and not automatons.

Success worth having has always been and always will be the result of clear goals, purposeful planning, follow-through, and appropriate adjustments.

And anything worth having is worth the time it takes to get it right.

Give People What They Want

More than anything, people want to be noticed.

You have many opportunities every day to make sure you give specific, positive feedback for the work that your team is putting into a task.

Make sure that when you give credit, that you give detailed examples of what people have done to contribute and clearly show how that helps the goals of the group.

Give specific feedback freely and frequently. Say it in front of the whole team, and pass the information up the chain of command, as appropriate.

You'll notice immediately how the people praised will continue to do what you recognized them for.

The old management axiom is right on the mark. "Behavior that's rewarded gets repeated."

Listen to What People Aren't Saying

You'll learn a whole lot more about what people are really thinking if you listen to how they say what they say and be less caught up in the actual words themselves.

Let's look at the fact that half the people you know are below average communicators. That's not an unkind remark. It's simply based on the definition of the word "average." Half are above; half are below.

When people are upset or emotional, their communication skills slip in direct proportion to how upset they are.

You will be a leader extraordinaire if you cultivate the quality of listening to the emotions behind the words.

I tell participants in my seminars on communications that communication is not the exchange of words, but the exchange of ideas and emotions.

Be the person who listens to what's not being said, but what is really meant. From there, you'll find yourself with information that will help you respond appropriately to almost any situation.

Deal with Problems Swiftly

Weak managers pretend problems will go away by themselves. Sometimes, they don't want to confront problem people ostensibly because they don't want to hurt their feelings.

Let me give you some tough love here. If you get caught up in the trap of not wanting to hurt people's feelings, then maybe you shouldn't have a leadership position.

Your team relies on you to quickly, fairly, and diplomatically handle problems.

If you don't take swift action, don't think for a second the problem will disappear. It may go underground, but believe me when I tell you it's still there. In the meantime, you are losing the respect of your team because you didn't face the issue head on.

Be brave and diplomatic, and get that situation in hand right now.

Deal with Problems Privately

Sometimes, a manager finally decides to face up to and address a problem, and then ends up giving negative feedback to a person in public.

Not a good idea! When this happens, there's a negative reverberation that affects everyone who witnessed the confrontation.

First, the person you corrected will feel either angry or humiliated. Not only have you failed to influence him, you've also put others in an uncomfortable position.

Second, the people listening feel embarrassed or angry on behalf of the person you've criticized. Even if they agree that the other person was in the wrong, no one wants to be part of another's "talking to."

And finally, you will have a long hard row to hoe to get back in good graces with any of these people. Reputations are so hard to develop and so easy to harm.

Privately deliver any corrections, criticisms, or bad news.

Address the Right Issue

When it's time to confront, make the confrontation about the problem and not the person.

Make it clear that you're talking about the specific behavior and give just a few examples.

Practice this beforehand. Only a novice leaves this to chance and tries to wing it when confronting someone about unacceptable behavior.

When you're practicing this, I recommend that you even write it out on paper or role-play with a trusted friend or advisor. Watch for any slips into vague comments or accidental name-calling.

Need an example of that last one? I had a participant in one of my leadership seminars who said she couldn't understand why her feedback to her boss didn't work. When she told me what she'd told her supervisor, my client said, "Well, I told her that I was frustrated when she raised her voice to me because it's unprofessional."

There you go. She recognized as soon as she'd said it that in this instant, she'd called her boss "unprofessional." It may be unprofessional behavior, but we are focused on the facts, and calling names won't do a thing for our own credibility. No matter what the other person is doing, you consistently want to address the right issue.

Say It and Zip It

When you're giving feedback that's tough to hear, it's more important than ever that you don't wear out your welcome by being too wordy.

Say what you want to say in as few words as possible to make your meaning clear and then zip it.

You are trying to persuade them to behave differently, and the more they feel that you're lecturing them, the less receptive they're going to be to the message you're trying to communicate.

Do remind yourself that when people are in the wrong they are even more sensitive to how much the other person is talking.

Your entire script should take about 30 seconds. Here's an example. And by the way, this is done in private: "Jean, I feel frustrated when you're late to our meetings. It holds us up and puts us behind in getting our meeting over in 30 minutes. Please be prompt next time."

Boom, you're done. If you like, you can even ask, "Can you help me understand why you've been late?" But that's up to you, because you know Jean a lot better than I, and you know if that question will fling open the door of excuse-making or not.

© Crystal Jonas

Words to Avoid: Always and Never

A s a leader, one of your most powerful tools to inspire and influence others is your credibility.

If people believe you, and if you know what you're talking about, if you consistently walk your talk and lead by example, they are inclined to believe you, they will allow you to influence them.

Two words that call into question your credibility are "always" and "never." Why? The reason is that all they need to do is find one exception, and your claim won't carry any weight at all.

Most importantly, be sure to avoid these two words when you are giving anyone constructive feedback, otherwise known as criticism. They are already going to want to tune you out. Any casual comment that includes "always" and "never" is likely to make them tune you out entirely.

For example, approaching a team member and saying, "Bob, you're always late" will immediately send his defenses up. And is he really, literally late absolutely every single day? Just one exception when he can prove you wrong is enough to negate your entire message.

Don't Combine Confrontation and Compliments

I cringed (I hope not visibly) when a participant in one of my Student Leadership workshops told me that her method for giving feedback is "Kiss, kick, kiss." She said she says something nice to them, gives it to 'em between the eyes, and closes with something nice.

Yikes! I respectfully disagree.

This method of feedback will make your team members constantly suspicious of you anytime you offer positive comments.

Another participant told me that his girlfriend doesn't even like for her boss to say nice things to her anymore because all day long, she waits for the other shoe to drop!

Because it's critical that you're clear, and essential that you praise good work immediately, you must make sure that criticisms are completely separate from compliments.

If you are constantly giving clear feedback, and giving lavish praise, you can feel good about the fact that corrective comments are necessary at times, and your feedback will not crush the spirit of the other person.

Watch "I'm Sorry" During Confrontation

When should you say, "I'm sorry"? Well, probably not as often as you are saying it.

Say it when you accidentally step on someone's toe, or when someone has experienced a loss. As in, "I'm sorry for your loss."

Do not say "I'm sorry" when you are giving constructive feedback. Let's say someone is consistently interrupting others during your weekly meetings.

First, you know, of course, that you'll be talking with the interrupter in private.

Second, you need to make clear that you need that person to respect the rights of others to speak their minds uninterrupted.

If you were to say at any time "I'm sorry" it could make the person to whom you're speaking think that you aren't confident in making this request.

"I'm sorry" should only be uttered when you are genuinely sorry about what happened.

Be Interested

You know that people don't care how much you know until they know how much you care.

The key to connecting with people is to be genuinely interested in what they have to say.

One of the most popular college programs I offer is called "Fitting in Fast: How to Adjust Quickly and Have a Great Social Life in College." People want to be able to adjust quickly and know that their peers accept them. They want to be an important part of the groups they join and volunteer their time to.

It seems so many people believe that the burden is on them to be sparkling conversationalists, so they struggle with what topics they'll discuss with people they've just met.

If you are one of those more quiet leaders that would like to form solid relationships with your team, you can do this quite easily.

The key is to be interested in what they are talking about. It's more important when forming relationships and bonds of respect if you are interested rather than interesting.

Motivate the Team to Understand Your Point of View

Before you push forward with your own ideas that you'd like your team to buy into, there is a profound action you can take to predispose them to listen to you and be receptive to your opinions.

Be sure that you are listening carefully to them and how they feel about the situation.

In Developing the Leader Within You John C. Maxwell quotes David Burns, a medical doctor and professor of psychiatry at the University of Pennsylvania who said:

"The biggest mistake you can make in trying to talk convincingly is to put your highest priority on expressing your ideas and feelings. What most people really want is to be listened to, respected, and understood. The moment people see that they are being understood, they become motivated to understand your point of view."

Listen, respect, and understand the ideas of others first. Then, they will be open to your ideas.

Let Them Know They Matter

Want your team to consistently bring their best work to the group? Let them know that their activities make a specific and measurable contribution to the mission of your group.

Organizational psychologists repeatedly point out that once workers' primary needs are met, and they have enough money to cover their basic needs and a bit more, they are working for more than just money.

People will continue to perform at peak levels in direct proportion to how much their unique contributions are valued and how those contributions make a specific positive impact on the team's results.

Tell them their work matters, and why. They'll love hearing it, and you'll love the results.

Cultivate the Talents and Strengths of Your Team

Many managers fail because they mistakenly believe that their team has to be good at everything.

Not so. Seek to help your team specialize in what they really enjoy as this more often than not coincides with what they naturally do well.

While other managers are floundering because they are trying to put square pegs into round holes you can be paying attention to where the strengths and interests of you team lie and assigning them duties where they will shine.

It's a myth that any one of us needs to be great at everything. Remember this fact for your own personal growth and professional development as well. Discover your own strengths and gifts and work at getting even better at where you're already quite good.

Such is a major element of success.

Be Calm and Confident

In times of crisis, your team will look to you to determine how to react.

If you remain calm and confident that your team will weather the storm, they will believe it, too.

Make sure you adopt your own personal strategies for maintaining physical calm in times of stress, as if these aren't readily available to you, when turbulence comes (and it will) you won't be ready to face it head on.

Here is my personal favorite deep breathing pattern to keep a level, logical head in times of stress:

Inhale through the nose for eight seconds.

Hold this for seven seconds.

Exhale for eight seconds.

Do this three times. Any more than that, and you may hyperventilate.

Deal Quickly and Fairly with Complaints

One issue people have with trusting their team leaders arises when they believe the leader isn't responding to their concerns.

You need to make sure that you listen carefully when someone issues a complaint. Ask them specifically what outcome they would like, and how they would like you to help to make that happen.

Deal with complaints as soon as you can. They do not go away on their own, and you will lose respect if you let the problem fester.

Again, you'll want to deal with all interpersonal conflict in private. It's important to not publicly announce to the group that someone is having a problem (more than half of the team doesn't even notice). You don't want to stir up trouble, but rather nip it in the bud.

Ask Their Opinion

People feel you respect them, their work, and their creative ideas when you ask their opinions.

The opposite behavior would be a controlling manager who is always presenting ideas about the exact way things should be done without the slightest regard for what others think.

Who will know better than the front line people about the way processes on the front line should be carried out?

Besides, lots of students may have purposefully chosen to be in your group because they want close involvement in projects they can add to their resumes. I teach students how to use their college experience to jumpstart their career success by doing just that.

It's fine for you to have a clear concept about what you want the goal to be. However, when you're deciding the best way to achieve that goal, ask for feedback from the people who will be carrying out the tasks that make that goal a reality.

Be Fair

There have been managers who will play favorites with some team members. They'll make allowances when those favorites are late, they'll give them the plumb assignments, they'll grant time off when everyone needs to push forward to achieve a goal.

If you want to maintain your credibility and your respect, you must treat everyone fairly. This may be a particular challenge if someone on your team is a close friend of yours.

Your group may take on a particularly challenging project, and you'll want the entire team to know your expectation that each member will be giving her or his best to complete this project as a team.

Take great caution to treat all team members the same. What you would say or do for one is what you would say and do for all. Nothing less is acceptable.

Expect the Best

Want to get top-notch attitudes and work products? Of course, you do.

Expect the best of people and let them know that you do. You will be delighted at how this faith in them will be rewarded.

Ralph Waldo Emerson wrote: "Trust men and they will be true to you; treat them greatly and they will show themselves to be great."

Think of someone who may have been hypercritical of you in the past. You're lucky if you can't think of a single person. If you can, recall how rarely you ended up truly being at your best around this person.

Now, imagine that person who always believed in the best in you. And that's what you gave them, isn't it?

Again, these students are working almost always on a volunteer basis; they can quit whenever they want. Sometimes, their reason for staying is that they feel valued and appreciated.

You are in a position to help others be who they are at their best simply by making it clear that you have faith in them and expect that they will be at their best.

Play to Your Own Strengths

Just because you're the leader of your group doesn't mean you need to be good at everything! Make sure you're playing to your strengths just as you will help your team members do.

We waste time and energy when we imagine that we have to do everything our team does and then some. Your job is to lead them, not to do the work for them. If there is a secondary duty that you believe should be performed, but you're not good at it, delegate that task to someone who will naturally be good at it.

Let's say that your team is putting on a fund raising event, and several organizations need to be called and asked to sponsor the program. You know that you aren't at all comfortable with that.

No problem. Find someone who would do well at this and get him or her on the project immediately. The worst thing you could do would be to procrastinate and wait until the last minute to get help.

William Gladstone wrote: "He is a wise man who wastes not energy on pursuits for which he is not fitted, and he is wiser still who from among the things he can do well, chooses and resolutely follows the best."

Start Your Day on a Win

No doubt, as a student you are one busy person.

It's interesting how some people get so much done and others seem constantly busy, yet have little to show for their efforts.

Here's how you can improve the quality and quantity of your daily output.

Mark down what you value, your goals, and your plans. Once you know your plans, make a list of things you need to do.

Each day, know exactly what actions you can take to get you closer to what you want. Start with one meaningful activity every single day of your life. Make sure that no matter what else occurs as the day unfolds, there will be at least one action that you have taken that you know is getting you closer to where you'd like to be.

Once you begin to practice this, you will experience the positive addiction of being productive every day of your life.

Follow Your Own Energy Bursts

As much as you can, control when you do things. Do brain-intensive activities when you're at your best, if you can work them around your other responsibilities.

Some of us are morning people, some don't even feel fully awake until around 10a.m. Others peak in energy later at night.

Whenever you can, arrange your classes, homework, and work in accordance to your own natural spurts of energy.

If you know that the time after lunch is typically a low energy ebb, do all you can to avoid meeting with your team during this time. Your own attitudes will influence your team's attitudes. You can imagine how ineffective a meeting would be when the person leading it is ready to take a nap!

By the way, if you typically do have a lull in energy after lunch, you may find it helpful to eat a lunch that maximizes brainpower and energy and that is high protein and low fat. And watch those refined carbohydrates, such as white bread, pasta, and mashed potatoes. They will put you into a carbo coma in no time!

Max Out Learning Opportunities

Did you know that a hallmark of successful people is that they keep learning? There's an old saying that "Successful people have big libraries and poor people have big TVs." Personally, I think really successful people have both.

Even after you're done with your formal education, continue to learn and grow.

If you want to be in the elite group of the truly successful, keep reading books, going to seminars, and listening to audios in your car.

I especially recommend that you use your time driving to listen to audios because that's time you're a captive audience anyway.

You may be so busy with class work that the thought of reading a book that will help you with professional development or personal growth is the furthest thing on your mind.

Listening while driving works for almost everyone and most people enjoy how it allows them to get smarter with no extra time involved.

Keep an Attitude of Service

Your role as a leader is really more about those you lead than you.

When you are helping others be who they are at their best, you can become focused on what you as a team can accomplish for a greater good.

There's a new way of looking at leadership that emphasizes the role of the "servant leader." That simply means that the leader is there to provide guidance and resources to the team members so they have everything they need to accomplish the mission.

In school, you are in a unique position to make a significant contribution to your school, community, and others in general. Make the most of this opportunity by making your work about making a difference.

Leader as focal point, and the ultimate ruler is long gone. Those leaders who stay tuned in to what their teams need and make sure they have those resources will accomplish much more on a consistent basis than any other kind of leader.

In his 1989 inaugural address, George W. Bush said, "There is but one use of power and it is to serve people."

Have an Elevated and Healthy Self-Image

You will never rise higher than your own opinion of yourself.

You may have been raised thinking that it's immodest or even annoying to others to hold yourself in high regard, but this is not so.

You don't have to strut around flaunting your greatness in front of others. Just hold that high opinion of yourself inside and appreciate that you have unique gifts with which you can serve others and make a profound difference in the world.

This is a healthy attitude that you will want to take with you as you embark upon your career and grow professionally. Remember that others will rarely give you more than you feel worthy of. I call this "raising your ego-stat."

Believe in yourself, you team, and your vision for your team. Be open to constant personal and professional improvement.

You must think well of yourself before you can think well of others and help them to excel.

Laugh!

Great leaders have a wonderful sense of humor. The ability to laugh at oneself and at circumstances is a much-appreciated gift.

Life can be a roller coaster ride, as you no doubt have figured out already!

Your team will respect that you don't take yourself too seriously when you are able to openly accept when you've "misfired" and can even see the humor in your mistake.

Laughter really is the best medicine. In fact, people who suffered from clinical depression were involved in an experiment where they were given no drugs at all. Instead, they had a half hour a day of laughter therapy. They would watch funny videos for 30 minutes every day.

At the end of the study the group that laughed had a more significant improvement in their symptoms than those who had medicine!

So laugh it up, learn, and move on.

Exercise

As a leader you need the physical stamina to go the extra mile. You wouldn't ask your team to do anything you wouldn't do yourself, right? And there are times when a lot will be expected of your team.

Make sure that you have the physical ability not only to keep up with the rest of your team, but also to make sure you are the "first in and last out." You lead your team from the front, and it's hard to do that if you're huffing and puffing to catch up with them.

Exercise, by the way, will help you have greater focus and attention in class and during your studies.

Exercise will not only give you a physical edge, it will give you a mental edge as well. People who have active lifestyles are better problem solvers and handle all forms of stress better.

Accentuate the Positive

People can't stand to be around negative people. You know who I mean those sad sacks, and whiners who often say they are just being realistic.

Phooey.

Psychologists proved long ago that we move toward what we think about and what we focus on expands. If you want positive outcomes, focus on positive outcomes.

If you want negativity, go for it. Just know that's exactly what you'll get in return.

One of the programs I deliver is called "Fitting in Fast: How to Adjust Quickly and Have a Great Social Life in College," we cover what attracts people to you and what turns them running in the opposite direction. Negativity is definitely one of those traits that sends them running away.

When faced with challenges, ask, "what's good about this is . . ." and fill in the blank. Don't give up until you have an answer. The challenge is there whether you find a way around it or not. You might as well put your millions of brain cells to work finding a smart solution to the situation.

Find the silver lining to every cloud.

Emerson wrote: "The measure of mental health is the disposition to find good everywhere."

Bounce!

Even as a young college student, you've lived long enough to experience disappointments.

It's been said that the measure of success is not how often you fall down, but how often you get up. Success boils down to getting up once more than you fall.

As a student of what makes people successful, I was surprised and actually encouraged when I discovered how often successful people failed. I suppose I thought that they were somehow special and rarely, if ever, failed. The opposite is true. They fail quite a bit.

The difference is that they always have a burning desire to succeed and they keep focused on what they are going for. This laser-guided focus, coupled with an ego strong enough to learn from their mistakes, and the stubbornness to get right back up again is what makes them successful.

If you follow that formula, there's no reason you can't enjoy the same level of success as anyone you admire.

Just remember that when life knocks you down, bounce right back up.

Develop a Passion for Personal Growth

To paraphrase the old saying, "no one can lead who is not master of himself."

Are you continually working on your personal growth plan? Are you thinking that you've made it and there's nothing else to learn?

Although I have a healthy degree of self-esteem, I say that unless this is as good as I'm going to get, I need to continually grow.

This means shining some light on those blind spots and working on the areas that might be holding you back in achieving your dreams.

If you aren't getting the results you want from your team or in your personal life, you might want to look within and discover where you might be able to strengthen those areas of weakness.

I suggest that you might want to start by asking someone who loves you enough to tell you the truth what one or two areas you could most tweak to get a better result in your personal or professional life.

If you'd like to look at what I've used, and in fact created myself, go to http://CrystalJonas.com.

Don't be an Island

Know how your team fits into the larger organization. Sometimes leaders have gotten so good at developing their team that they start to inadvertently develop an empire mentality. That's where the team and the leader are an end in themselves and not there to serve the bigger picture.

You can use the main mission as a positive way to motivate team members. Show them exactly how your team fits within the larger organization's purpose.

To do this, it's important that you can clearly express the intent behind the organization's mission statement. And please, don't even bother quoting it. So many of those are hard to remember and even harder to understand.

If you can boil down the essence of that big picture and show your team their part in making that all come together, you can motivate your team and remind them of their bigger purpose.

Honestly Assess Your Individual Progress

In my program for college students called "How to Lead So Others Will Follow" we cover the topic "How to deal with people with toxic personalities." I guess I don't have to tell you how awkward it is when the team leader is the one with the toxic personality!

Make sure you're not the one everyone else sees as toxic. Here's a sure sign to tell you that you might be the negative person others are trying to deal with. If, when something goes wrong, you always find someone else to blame, or a circumstance outside your control to put the fault on, you just might need to take a closer look at yourself before you try to start fixing other people.

The people who are the problem people take no responsibility for how well they do or don't get along with others. It's always the other person's fault. Trust me, it's hard to be around people who don't have the ego to face up to their own shortcomings.

On your path to be who you are at your best you've got to be willing to look honestly at where your weaknesses are and what you can do to strengthen them.

If you aren't willing to face up to your shortcomings, you can't expect any one on your team would acknowledge theirs.

Admit Errors

A sign of low self-esteem is when people cannot or will not admit when they've made a mistake. You've seen it at work. These people will go out of their way to justify their choices even when it's clear that those were the wrong choices.

Or worse yet, they will attempt to blame others for their mistakes.

If someone is blaming you and you had nothing to do with what happened, direct them to the right person.

For example, let's say that someone is chewing you out because the budget failed to include a critical category. You can say, "Please call Chris at extension 4589 and ask him why he chose to omit that."

While it's important for your reputation to quickly admit your mistakes and correct them as best you can, there's no reason to take responsibility for errors that aren't yours.

Tell Them When the Going is Getting Tough

In my program "How to Lead So Others Will Follow" we cover what people expect of you in times of crisis.

People dislike being kept in the dark. It encourages speculation, gossip, and hard feelings if your team senses that something is up and you aren't being straightforward with them.

There may be times when you can't give complete information, or you just don't know all the facts. Your team will appreciate it if you're open with them about this fact.

Say, "Here's what I do know (or what I can tell you) and as soon as I can, I'll tell you more."

Be open when it's going to get turbulent and if you can, tell them when it's going to get better. Although no one likes bad news, they will appreciate that they have some control over the situation because now they have a bit more information and aren't being left in the dark.

Let Them Know They Belong

A fundamental need of all people is the need to belong. We want to feel important and that we have a place in the group. How you can help others feel important, and comfortable around you is covered in the program "Fitting in Fast: How to Adjust Quickly and Have a Great Social Life in College."

Without knowing it, many groups develop a cliquish mentality. You're in the "in" crowd or on the outside looking in. Unfortunately, it's not a phenomenon left behind in high school.

Make sure that all members take part in discussions and activities. It may be that you need to reign in some of the more vocal people to make sure that the more quiet members have an opportunity to speak up.

You'll want to give your team a heads up before any meeting so they know what's on the agenda and what ideas you'd like them to bring to the table.

Know that some people are naturally introverted and do not like to be put on the spot in a meeting. So, while it's important that you include everyone, create a setting that's comfortable for all different personality types to share in the discussion.

Feed Their Five Needs

If you give people what they need personally, they will be at their best professionally.

I've boiled this down to five basic needs. To make it easy, they start with the five vowels.

People have a need to be **a**ppreciated. Recognize people for whatever unique talents they offer. Their best really is good enough.

S**e**e them as exceptional. It's important for people to know that they have something to offer that not everyone does. If they can see how their contributions are theirs alone, they will be less likely to slack off and let down the team.

Include them in the decision making process. Ask their opinion on the best way to get the job done.

Ackn**o**wledge that they are one of a kind. This is especially important if they bring you a problem. Acting as though everyone has the same problem can make them feel as if you're trivializing it.

Understand them. More than being agreed with, people what to feel understood. Listen carefully and ask for as much clarification as necessary for you to fully understand where they're coming from.

Squash Gossip

If you want to lose trust quickly, you'll not only allow gossip to take place in front of you, you'll take part in it, or even initiate it.

To clarify, gossip refers to talking about another person, whether or not they're part of the group or present.

Make it clear that you aren't comfortable talking about someone without their being present and giving their side of the story.

Might you be seen as a goody-goody if you do this? Well, maybe so. But more importantly, you'll be quickly admired, respected, and trusted as someone who would not take advantage of another person's absence.

Act Confidently, Especially During Times of Change

Never is your ability to exercise and demonstrate strong leadership more needed than when your team is experiencing rapid change. It could be that it is change that you initiated; it could be major change that no one wanted in the first place. Whatever the circumstances, your team is looking to you for guidance. Be strong. They will be watching.

Act confidently that all will go well, and any blips will be dealt with quickly and competently.

You likely need your team's best work during these times of change and they will be much more likely to perform at their peak if their guidance from you is one of confidence and strength.

When you show your confidence, your nonverbal communication cues will speak even more loudly than your words, so make sure your behavior supports your words.

Trust Your Team and Get Out of Their Way

Your attitude of complete confidence in your team's willingness and ability to give their best to any endeavor will ensure they will be at their best even when you aren't present.

Dr. Pierce P. Brooks, author of How Power Selling Brought Me Success in 6 Hours said that when he wants people to do something, he finds a personal reason why they'd want to do it, then assumes they will do it.

Dr. Brooks remarked, "I let them know I believe they can do it, that I have confidence in their ability, that I trust them to do a good job—then leave them alone and let them do it. Constantly looking over a man's shoulder implies that you do not quite trust him to do a good job. I assume that he is going to do a good job, and I'm seldom disappointed."

Make sure you're not standing over their shoulder every step of the way once their work is underway.

Don't Project a Poor Self-Image by Accident

Does the behavior of someone in your organization drive you crazy? Is she insensitive or crabby? Is he boastful and selfish?

Measure carefully the words you use to talk about others. First, obviously, it will lead anyone within the sound of your voice to wonder if you'd speak ill of them if they weren't present.

And secondly, you must know that what you say about others says more about you than it does about them.

Know that psychologists have told us for ages that what bothers us most in someone else reflects our own shortcomings.

Turn your annoyance with someone else into an opportunity to become more self-aware about a quality you could tweak.

Speak Up, Speak Out, Speak Often

Here's another great tip that will help you not only in school but also as you pursue professional success.

The highest paid skill is the ability to orally communicate. Your ability to inspire others to motive themselves to be consistently at their best is what will set you apart from others in the field of leadership.

The best way to get good at speaking is to take every single opportunity you have to do so.

This means, speak in meetings with peers, offer to facilitate workshops, and speak to local service organizations about any aspect of leadership. By the way, your community will have several, or even dozens of, service organizations and will welcome you to come speak. Check your local paper for these meetings and call the person who is the point of contact. She or he will tell you with whom you can iron out the details.

And be sure to keep track of all of these engagements, so you can include them on your resumes. Your future employer is going to love knowing that you can communicate well!

The more you practice, the more quickly you improve this essential skill.

Know What Positive Thinking Is, and Isn't

I'm a firm believer in your ability to positively impact the attitudes and results of your team by modeling a positive attitude.

I have to say, though, that positive thinking has gotten a bad rap because some people don't really understand what it is, and what it isn't.

Positive thinking is staying focused on what you do want. That's the positive part. Your concentration on what you do want as opposed to what you don't want.

Some people mistakenly believe that positive thinking means you don't acknowledge challenges in your path of getting what you want.

If you don't acknowledge those challenges, you aren't likely to be able to solve them and get them out of your way so you can continue on your path to what you do want.

We're teleological, and we move toward what we think about. Keep a clear picture of your goals right in front of you and you'll be able to quickly overcome any roadblocks that arise.

Be Aware that Most People Don't Like to Be Kidded

Although there are a small number of thick-skinned people out there who don't mind it, you must realize that most people do not like to be kidded.

Think about it. You're usually kidding them because of a habit or point of view that's different from the rest of the group.

While it's true that people like to be seen as one of a kind, they want it to be perceived as a good quality that sets them apart from others.

Otherwise, people want to be included and to be considered part of a group. They will feel self-conscious, embarrassed, and perhaps excluded if they are kidded.

This is something even your friends won't tell you, so if you tend to kid people, you need to know that most people really don't care for that at all.

By the way, saying "I was just kidding" doesn't lessen the blow.

Use "White Magic" to Connect with People

Les Giblin, the author of How to Have Confidence and Power in Dealing with People suggested that each of us is "running for office" every day. People we meet and interact with are constantly sizing us up and determining whether to find us believable or not.

He recommends that to positively influence others, we follow the advice of Oliver Wendell Holmes who gave the following advice for the best way to get elected to office.

"To be able to listen to others in a sympathetic and understanding manner is perhaps the most effective mechanism in the world for getting along with people and tying up their friendship for good. Too few people practice the white magic of being good listeners."

Listening well captures the attention of people faster than being a smooth talker.

Convince Quickly

When you're leading your team, you don't always have much extra time to think about how to move forward on your next project. Sometimes, you need to get people on board quickly and then move on from there.

You get people to sign off on your ideas not because it's an important idea to you, but because you've clearly shown how going along with your concept harmonizes with what's important to them.

To find out what people value, once again we return to the idea of being a great listener.

People will tell you in moments what's important to them. They may talk about their family, or academic interests, financial concerns, or their ideal job, or where they're from.. As you are listening, you will quickly discover what their hot buttons are.

Your challenge is in finding a way that their supporting your ideas clearly supports the values that they hold close.

You convince quickly by keeping their goals in mind.

Work with Ego to Convince Them

Years ago, two professors from New York University's Speech Department studied 10,000 real life arguments over a seven-year period. They listened to husbands and wives, corporate salespeople and counter clerks, politicians and U.N. delegates. They wanted to know who won the most arguments and why.

Overwhelmingly, the people who "convinced" others most often were the people who lead the people they were trying to convince to convince themselves.

Rather than trying to beat down the other person, poke holes in their arguments, and generally try to win by "one upping" the other person (as professional debaters try to do), the successful convincers cultivated the good will of the other person and helped them come to the desired outcome as though it were their own idea.

So back off, don't bully, and lead by asking them questions that will allow them to convince themselves.

Praising Ability Increases Ability

A renowned concert violinist has taught little children to play the violin, widely considered to be the most difficult instrument to learn, solely by positive reinforcement.

It seems we have an innate desire and ability to want to do well and to be able to do well when we are properly led.

Psychologist Henry H. Goddard wanted to measure the impact of positive statements on the energy of children.

In an experiment the proctor said before administering the test, "You will have little trouble with this test. It is well within your abilities and intelligence." This comment resulted in much higher marks than when the children were given negative messages about their ability to do well on the same test.

Clearly, you get what you expect of people.

Praise the Attitude or Attribute, Not the Person

This critical point is covered in depth when I deliver my college program "Fitting in Fast: How to Adjust Quickly and Have a Great Social Life in College" with the topic "How to make people feel comfortable with you quickly."

Be as specific as you possibly can when you give praise. This is because you clarify in their subconscious mind what they're doing well, and behavior that's rewarded gets repeated.

If you say, "You're really nice." That's way too vague to ensure the behavior will be repeated. After all, what behavior is being complimented?

If you say, "You handled that upset person with grace and respect. Your approach calmed him down quickly. I admire your patience."

Now that's clear.

Also, specific references sound genuine and all compliments need to be not only specific, but also honest.

Articulate Measurable Areas of Improvement

At one time or other, your duties as a leader will call on you to give constructive feedback.

I admit, this can be a little tricky with volunteers. Remember, though, whether you lead volunteers, or paid employees, your respect for them will always get you a lot further than trying to force them to do something because you're the boss.

You've already read about not sandwiching bad news between good news. This makes the message confusing and frustrates the person listening.

Regardless of the behavior you want them to stop doing, you want to be quite clear about what you want them to start doing. In fact, make a date in the near future, say about a week, when you will get back with them about how they're coming so far.

The more specific and detailed you can be about what you want and when you want it, the more likely you are to get the behavior changes you're looking for.

Ask for Corrections, Don't Demand Them

Nothing annoys followers more than a manager who throws her weight around. More than anything, this reveals uncertainty on the manager's part and a low sense of self-esteem; not exactly qualities people admire.

When people feel confident that what they're requesting is fair, they don't go around making demands of others.

Remember that you will be a much more convincing persuader if you get those people to see what's in it for them when they change the way they're doing things. If you're listening carefully when they speak, you'll know what's important to them and be able to get a stronger commitment to your request for changes.

Help Them Set Specific Goals

Studies have revealed that you will accomplish much more when you have specific goals than if you have vague ideas about what you'd like to accomplish.

One of the weakest forms of "guidance" would be to tell people "do your best." We all need clear-cut, specific objectives with a deadline for achieving them.

Once those objectives have been agreed on, you can decide how much involvement you need to take in helping them to plan the process for reaching their goals.

If you have a high performance team, they will likely be good at setting their own benchmarks along the way.

Either way, you can have planned progress reports at pre-announced times so everyone knows how the big picture is fitting together, and so you can make minor adjustments as needed.

Know and Use the Prime Motivator

Your team is motivated primarily by recognition. Ways to do this are covered more completely in my program "How to Lead So Others Will Follow" in the section called "How to bring out the best in other people."

How each person wants to receive such recognition is up to him or her. Some people who are introverted prefer not to have a big fuss made at the main meeting in front of everyone. On the other hand, gregarious extroverts would not feel as valued if you took them aside privately to thank them. They prefer for the whole group to witness their accolades.

In his book, *The Truth About Managing People . . .And Nothing But the Truth*, Stephen P. Robbins noted that a recent study found that among a list of common motivators, personal thanks from a manager for a job well-done is the most motivating. Sadly, he reported, more than 58% of people responding to this survey said their managers typically did not give such praise.

Recognition is highly valued by the people receiving it, yet it costs next to nothing to give.

Fulfill Promises

Do you keep your commitments? When you say you're going to hold a 30-minute meeting on your groups next big project, does it start and end on time with you well prepared to facilitate it?

When you say you're going to follow up with someone about an issue, do you do so?

Can people count on you to be prompt? Remember, you must value the time of others by being punctual.

If you cannot keep your small promises, like being on time and following through, there's no reason for people to believe you'll keep the larger promises.

Your word is your bond. Your actions, more than anything you say, will influence whether people perceive you as credible.

Encourage and Respect Differences

One of your biggest assets in your team is the fact that your team is made up of a group of unique personalities. Each person has had a unique set of experiences and comes to the team with his or her own ideas for the best way to get the job done.

Make sure you find a way to respect this aspect of individuality as you bring these diverse people together for your common goals.

Beware of "groupthink," where the members of the team abandon their individual ideas and quickly jump on the same bandwagon. In such a situation, team members agree too soon about a solution that's far too simplistic and ineffective.

You can encourage "out of the box" thinking and synergy by instituting recurring brainstorming sessions whenever it's time to problem solve. Let your team know that during such a session, there's no judgment (that comes later) and that some of the most off-the-wall ideas will be the best.

Don't Interrupt an Introvert

Introverts speak seldom. They are thoughtful, quiet, and don't speak up until they have something to say. When they talk pay attention and listen. Don't be concerned if you're busy at the moment, because what they have to say is brief and to the point.

Since they seldom speak, it puts them off to be pushed aside or interrupted, and they won't often bother to approach you on the same topic later.

Also, make sure this person has an opportunity to talk at meetings. The more chatty types are likely to run right over the introverts. So moderate the conversations.

There's a section in my "Fitting in Fast" program that's especially for people who can be shy when meeting new people. Being shy isn't a character flaw, it's just a personality trait. No problem, you can work within your own unique style and still get along with all different kinds of people.

Temper the Extroverts

In "Fitting in Fast" the program covers how to make people feel comfortable with you quickly, we cover specifically the four main personality types and how to adjust when you're with each one, so you can quickly make friends and get along well with others.

Contrary to the introvert, an extrovert thinks out loud and tends to use many more words than an introvert does.

The extroverts, who have extreme tendencies, must be tempered and you'll need to set boundaries with them.

Especially important is to watch group dynamics and to make sure your extroverts are giving the introverts an opportunity to express their opinions.

You may need to quietly draw the extrovert aside and let her know that, in the interest of time and giving everyone an opportunity to speak, you're going to limit the time and frequency that each person can speak.

Then hold yourself to that. As someone who gives frequent seminars to corporations and schools on communication, I can guarantee that the person who talks too much is annoying those who don't get to talk enough.

Don't Waste the Time of Others

Brian Tracy reported a survey of CEOs who stated that half of meetings are unnecessary and the other half are twice as long as they need to be.

It's one thing to waste our own time, it's rude to waste someone else's.

Why are so many meetings a waste of time? In brief, they don't have clear focus, a firm start and stop time, and the people involved aren't clear on what's expected of them.

Here's what you can do to make your meetings more effective:

Have a clear-cut agenda

Stick to your start and stop times and don't begin again when someone comes in late.

Let people who will need to talk know where they are on the agenda and what's expected of them.

Only have people whose presence is needed attend the meeting.

If you have chatty types, keep everyone (yes, that's everyone) on an egg timer. When the time's up, they're finished. Let them know that you'll be doing this ahead of time, as they may want to practice to get it all in on time.

Cultivate Charisma

Your ability to communicate effectively is your most precious asset. Continually work on it and you will always reap the benefits of constant improvement.

I'll leave you with this final tip from a book I referenced earlier called *The Truth About Managing People. . . And Nothing But the Truth* by Stephen R. Robbins.

Robbins notes that you can become charismatic by following this three-step process:

Maintain optimism and use passion to generate enthusiasm.

Create a bond that inspires others to follow you.

Tap into the emotions of your followers and bring out their potential.

Read all you can about leadership and communication.

Keep learning and you will continue to inspire others to be who they are at their best.

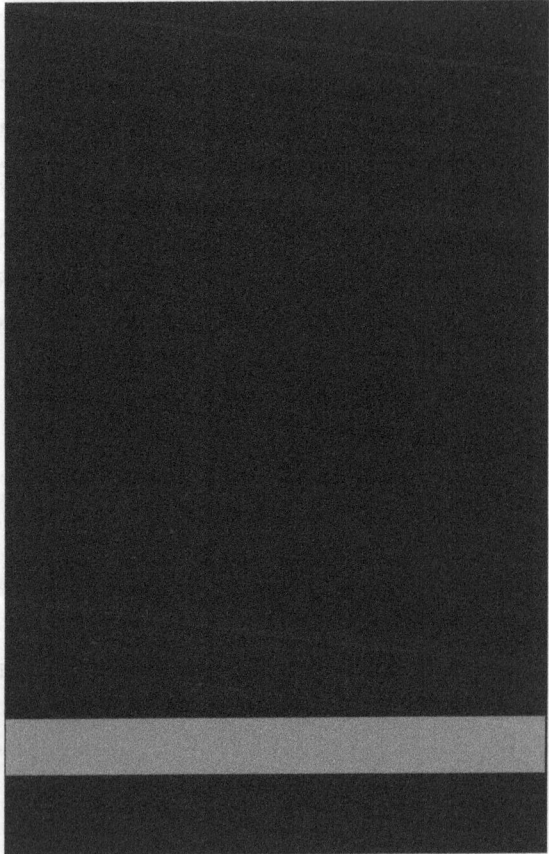

www.ingramcontent.com/pod-product-compliance
Lightning Source LLC
Chambersburg PA
CBHW061754020426
42331CB00006B/1484